A Story to Tell

40 DAY FOCUS ON YOUR WALK WITH GOD

By Jeffrey A. Johnson II, M.Div

[signature]

God Bless

PREACH:DOC

www.PreachDoc.com

Dedication

I dedicate *A Story to Tell*, my first book, to my father, Jeffrey A. Johnson, Sr., from whom I learned how important stories are in shaping our lives, and whose own story, lived daily before me, has shaped my life and drawn me to God.

Copyright ©2017 Jeffrey A. Johnson, II
PreachDoc Publishing
P.O. Box 18622
Indianapolis, Indiana USA 46218
www.PreachDoc.com

Cover Design by Tyler Hill
Book Production by Vision Communications

ISBN 978-0-9986696-1-8
Printed in the United States of America

Contents

Foreword

In this awesome book *A Story to Tell*, Jeffrey Johnson II follows in the footprints of Jesus by using stories, illustrations and anecdotes to help us to grasp some of God's most profound truths. Jesus is the greatest story teller. He told stories that were interesting, relevant, insightful and timeless. Most of all, the stories Jesus told were extremely enlightening as they revealed the truths of God which are not always easy to understand. However, Jesus' picture perfect portraits of God's life-giving principles helps us to see those principles very clearly.

Now Jeffrey Johnson II, like Jesus, tells some of the most simple, everyday experiences to unlock the wonderful mysteries of God's Word. He uses the art of storytelling at its highest level to help us to understand the powerful principles of God. This amazing book makes it possible for us to get closer to the Lord through meditation and daily devotions.

I am convinced, you will be enlightened, informed and inspired by Jeffrey Johnson's spirit-inspired imagination through these spiritual, beautiful and useful stories. Jeffrey Johnson, II, indeed has "A Story to Tell".

~ *Jeffrey A. Johnson, Sr.*

Introduction

Stories make a lasting impression on us. We will remember stories more easily than anything else. Matthew 13:34 says, "Jesus spoke all these things to the crowd in parables; He did not say anything to them without using a parable." Jesus knew the impact of a story, so He used stories to help people learn about God. In Luke 15, Jesus used three stories in a row to help people understand who God is. The parables or stories of the lost coin, the lost sheep, and the lost son, all illustrate how valuable we are to God and the passionate way He seeks for us when we are lost.

Jesus understood how powerful stories can be. Stories can help make complex ideas simple so that we can grasp the concepts. The stories of others can also encourage us as we continue to live out our own life stories. Think about it, we all have a story. In fact, our individual stories are intertwined with the stories of humankind throughout history. The decisions we make in our personal stories influence the stories of others. For example, the story of how many Europeans used Africans as their slaves explains how my ancestors first arrived in America. The many stories of those who participated in the Civil Rights Movement explain how others and I have had the opportunities we have had to succeed in this country. The story of my parents explains how my brothers and I came into being. Although we all have individual stories, our stories collectively influence one another in a powerful way.

A Story to Tell is a collection of stories, illustrations and anecdotes, that I hope will help you find direction in life, while drawing closer to God in your everyday living. As you read one brief story for each of the next forty days, my prayer is that these stories will help you better understand the story of Jesus and how relevant it is for today. My prayer is that God will use these stories to help enhance your own life story. My prayer is that the lessons found in these stories will help you in your relationship with God and your relationship with others. My prayer is that the stories told in this book will encourage you to tell your own story, so that others might learn from you about how Jesus can transform our lives for the better. Enjoy, my friends.

Inside Out

*When they came to Jesus, they saw the man who
had been possessed by the legion of demons,
sitting there, dressed, and in his right mind; and
they were afraid. (Mark 5:15)*

There is a man who came home from work one day and
discovered that his chimney and part of his roof had been
destroyed. A woman he met online didn't like the fact that he
wanted to break things off with her after only a few dates, so
she went to confront him. She found, however, that he wasn't at
home and all the doors and windows were locked. She couldn't
get inside the house to wait for him there. Desperate to get in,
the young woman climbed on the roof to slide through the
chimney in the spirit of Old Saint Nick. However, she got stuck
half way down. A neighbor called the authorities after hearing
the screams from the woman. The authorities arrived and failed
in several attempts to pull her out of the chimney. They decided
then that the only way they would be able to free her was by
destroying the chimney. The man came home from work and
discovered his chimney, roof and other components lying in a
heap on the ground. Everything came apart on the outside of
his home because there was something on the *inside* that didn't
belong.

Whatever we have on the inside of us has a way of manifesting itself on the outside. What we see in the physical is only a reflection of the spiritual. Maybe the reason why things are falling apart in our lives is because we are dealing with the physical manifestation of such things as: fear, low self-esteem, baggage from the past, and anxiety. Perhaps this is why our relationships, friendships, finances, and communities are constantly falling apart. Maybe what we are experiencing is the physical manifestation of the fear, negativity, and wrong thinking that is so prevalent in our hearts and minds. It is time to rid ourselves of all that doesn't belong on the inside and fill our hearts and minds instead with the Spirit of Christ. The man in Mark 5 was able to be freed of his demons after having a true encounter with Jesus, because Jesus always has what it takes to bring healing from the inside out. Too often, we run to *external* tools such as sex, social media, drugs, or alcohol to deal with *internal* issues. We need instead to run to this same Jesus who has the power to transform us from the inside out. Even in this moment, we can each look at something in our own life that is broken and ask Jesus to bring healing and transformation so that we can be whole from the inside out.

Leave the Losers, Roll with the Winners

After He put them all out, He took the child's father and mother and the disciples who were with him, and went in where the child was. (Mark 5:40)

In 2010, professional basketball player LeBron James left the Cleveland Cavaliers to play in Miami, Florida for the Miami Heat. Many people hated on LeBron James for that move. However, by leaving Cleveland, LeBron put himself in a position to win three NBA championships. As much as he may have cared about the people surrounding him in Cleveland, he felt that they didn't have what it would take to help him get to where he wanted to go. So he left his teammates behind there and connected with Pat Riley, Dwayne Wade and others who already had NBA championships under their belts. LeBron James taught us all a lesson. Sometimes, in order to reach certain goals and dreams, there are some people that we need to leave behind and others with whom we need to connect.

In Mark 5, Jesus shows us that in order to get things done, there are certain people from whom we need to detach, and certain people to whom we need to attach. In an attempt to raise a dead child, Jesus kicked out people who were hindering what He was trying to do and attached himself to others who had the child's best interest at heart. There are moments in life when God will require us to remove ourselves from certain people who hold us back from our greatness, dreams, and aspirations. Then there will be other moments in life that God will bring people in our lives who will give us the motivation, inspiration and wisdom to walk into our destiny. God will give us the discernment necessary to tell the difference between who we need to let go and who we need to let in. Leave the losers. Roll with the winners. Let God decide.

God is With You

Even though I walk through the darkest valley; I will fear no evil, for you are with me. (Psalm 23:4)

I had boarded a plane from Atlanta, where I was in seminary, to fly to Indianapolis to visit my family. As I was waiting for other passengers to board, I noticed a man getting onboard who had his hands full. He was carrying his duffle bag over his shoulder, while pulling another bag *and* carrying his baby daughter. As he was struggling trying to find his seat, the flight attendant approached to assist him. In her attempt to help this young man get to his seat, she took the child and began to walk backwards down the aisle to guide the father to his seat. However, as soon as the baby left the arms of her father, she began to cry, scream, and yell. Even though this baby couldn't understand what was happening, she knew that wherever she was going, she needed to be with her father. Once the father got himself situated and took the baby back in his arms, the child went from crying to smiling. She was now reconnected with her father, and her world felt right once again. It didn't matter to her where she was going, as long as she was going with her father.

Sometimes life has a way of separating us from our heavenly Father. Just as the baby in our story was never out of her father's sight, we are never out of our Father's sight. But she experienced a few moments in which she was being carried backwards, and she felt that she was moving away from him, so she panicked. Whenever we become separated from the Father, we can't help but go backwards. Living life away from the Father will have us going backwards in relationships, friendships, money management, and other avenues in life. A backwards life can cause us to cry out in frustration and fear. But the Father will never leave us in that chaotic situation alone. Today, King David reminds us that regardless how dark it gets in our lives, we have a Father in heaven that will never leave us alone. Remember, God is with you.

Level by Level

*Joseph was thirty years old when he entered
the service of Pharaoh.*

(Genesis 41:46)

Life sometimes reminds me of the video game Mario. Before Madden and 2K, there was Mario on the original Nintendo. The goal for Mario was to save Princess Peach from Bowser. In order to save the princess, Mario had to conquer level by level. There was no saving the princess on the last level without first going through level one. In moving through the game, the player discovered that the higher the level, the more difficult the game became. The higher the level the more obstacles and enemies there were to face. However, each level prepared the player for the next, and equipped him or her to get the ultimate victory.

The story of Joseph teaches us that dreams don't come true overnight; they come true over time. Joseph was seventeen years old when he had a dream of becoming great and powerful, but the Bible says he didn't live it out until he was thirty. This microwave society that we have created for ourselves wants everything to happen instantly — from relationships and friendships to careers and wealth. If things don't happen as quickly as we would like, we give up on them. But God doesn't work on our timetable and most often God takes us to our destiny level by level. We can't expect for God to elevate us to a higher level in our relationships, jobs, finances, and dreams when we can't properly handle the level we are already on. We can't expect for God to make us CEO of the company when all we do is surf through social media while we are on the clock. We can't expect for God to give us millions of dollars when we can't manage the few pennies that we have now. We can't expect for God to walk us into a healthy relationship when we think it's okay to sleep with anyone we choose. There are levels to our destiny, and life has a way of giving us more obstacles and challenges as we begin to pursue our purpose. We must understand that success and greatness don't happen overnight. They happen over time. Continue to trust God over time and watch God take you from faith to faith and from glory to glory. Understand that there are levels to reaching our destiny. Be patient level by level.

Put the Father in Your Corner

Father, I thank you that you have heard me. I knew that you always hear me, but I said these for the benefit of the people standing here, that they may believe that you sent me.

(John 11:41-42)

Floyd "Money" Mayweather went 49-0 in his boxing career. One of the reasons why Mayweather is undefeated is because of who he chose as his trainer. After each round of the fight, the boxer goes to his corner and gets assistance from the trainer. Whether it's a word of encouragement, a reminder of the game plan, or attention to the cuts the boxer received during the fight, the trainer gives the boxer what he needs to endure the blows of the opponent and go on to the next round. What set Mayweather apart from any other boxer was that his trainer was his father. So after every round of the fight Mayweather went to the corner to meet with his father, and it's his father who gave him what he needed to endure and come out with the victory. Now, Mayweather's father wasn't perfect and there were periods of estrangement between the two, but the undefeated champion credits his father with teaching him to fight and said that he wouldn't have become the winner that he is had it not been for his father.

In the fight of life, we need to make a Money Mayweather move and ensure that we have our heavenly Father in our corner. Life has a way of taking the best out of us. In those moments, we have to make sure we have the right people in our corner. It's good to have our parents, family, and best friends in our corner. But the most important move we can make is to be sure that God is in our corner. Unlike human fathers He *is* perfect and He never messes up nor abandons us. Our Father has the word, power and Spirit we need to endure the cuts and punches of life. We need to take some time after each round, whether good or bad, and have a moment with our heavenly Father because He has what it takes to give us the victory. Let's put the Father in our Corner.

The Power of the Word

How can a young man stay on the path of purity? By living according to your Word. (Psalm 119:9)

My friend Tyler Joshua Green reminded me of rapper J. Cole's first studio album, *Cole World: Sideline Story.* J. Cole shares the time when he first got word that he would be signed to hip-hop legend, Jay-Z. J. Cole says that he was in the car with his friends when he received a phone call informing him of the exciting news that he was Jay-Z's newest artist. J. Cole recalls that as he and his friends were celebrating the good news, he noticed the police were behind him pulling them over. He testifies that he was driving with a suspended license and expired plates, so as a result he got arrested and had to spend the night in jail. After receiving the word that he would be signed, J. Cole ended up getting locked up. However, J. Cole states that it was the easiest night anybody could do in jail—because he got word from Jay-Z before he experienced bondage that his life would be changed forever.

In our life's journey, there will be times when our lives don't align with the Word that we heard from God. The Word says that God will provide all of our needs, but in reality we don't have enough money to get through the week. The Word says that everything will work out for good, but in reality our situation is terrible. The Word says, I'm more than a conqueror in Christ Jesus, but in reality things aren't working out. But if J. Cole has a enough faith to take Jay-Z at his word to get him through his situation, then how much more do you and I, as children of God, need to take God at *His* word even when our world is falling apart? Society will try everything in its power to get us to stray away from the Word of God, but we've got to have enough faith to stand on the Word even when our world is crumbling. We have to continue to stand on the promises of God, because there is power in the Word.

Paid It All

Knowing that you were ransomed from the futile ways inherited from your forefathers, not with perishable things such as silver or gold, but with the precious blood of Christ, like that of a lamb without blemish or spot.

(1 Peter 1:18-19)

My family and I were blessed to take a vacation to Hawaii one year. On our way back to Indianapolis, we were stuck at a Hawaiian airport for hours. As we waited for our flight, we all wanted to connect to the Wi-Fi to pass the time. To my disappointment, there was a price attached to the Wi-Fi Internet. As I contemplated the decision to purchase, I noticed my younger brother Josiah (KJ) had already connected to the Wi-Fi Internet. KJ was surfing social media, streaming music and FaceTiming his homie at the same time. I quickly discovered that my brother had already paid the price to connect. So without hesitation, I asked my brother for the email and password he used to connect his devices to the Wi-Fi Internet. He generously shared the info with me. Once I was connected, I gave the info to my two other brothers, Jordan and Jalon, who shared that same info with our parents. Now the whole family was able to experience the power of being connected to the higher power, because we had a brother who was willing to pay the price.

Back on Calvary, Jesus paid the price of sin so that we can all connect to God, the Higher Power. Because Jesus paid this price of sin, we can connect with God just as we are. Regardless of our past mistakes, shortcomings and mess-ups, we still have the opportunity to engage in a personal relationship with God. Going to church doesn't connect us, wearing suits doesn't connect us; nor does quoting scriptures connect us to God. The only way for us to connect to the Higher Power is by putting our faith and trust in our Big Brother Jesus Christ, who has truly *paid it all*.

Christ Pleaser

Am I now trying to win the approval of human beings, or of God? Or am I trying to please people? If I were trying to please people, I would not be a servant of Christ. (Galatians 1:1)

I remember when members of my family got together to support my younger cousin, Lil Ty, in one of his first youth basketball games at Eastern Star Church. Lil Ty was so excited that his family had come to support him. Before the game he came over to us in the stands and predicted how well he and his team were going to do. He went on and on about how many points, rebounds, and steals he was going to get as he would lead his team to victory. Once the game started, Lil Ty was so excited when he got the ball that, instead of staying focus on the game, he would look into the stands at the crowd to make sure his family was watching. Unfortunately, the more Lil Ty was focused on us in the crowd, the more he began to run out of bounds, turn the ball over, and miss open teammates and open shots. The more he was concerned with the crowd, the more he missed out on the opportunity to experience victory.

Many of us tend to miss out on our dreams, aspirations, and the things that God has for us in life because we shift our focus from Christ to the crowd. The thoughts and opinions of the crowd seem to change with the wind. One minute the crowd praises us, the next they campaign to crucify us. Individuals who live their lives to please the crowd will never be the persons whom God has called them to be. They are too focused on what others think and how to attract the most "likes" — even from people they don't know. They dress, behave, and make choices based on what will win approval from the masses. Likes from the crowd will never compare to the love that Christ has for us. We need to take our attention away from the crowd and put it on Christ. Then we will see victory show up in our lives. We need to be Christ pleasers, not people pleasers.

You Need To Cut It

In the year King Uzziah died, I saw the Lord. (Isaiah 6:1)

In the movie *127 Hours*, James Franco plays the real-life Aron Ralston, an adventurous outdoorsman and mountain climber. While hiking alone through Blue John Canyon in Utah, he slipped while climbing down a canyon wall and fell before having his arm pinned to a wall by a boulder. He was stuck for a 127 hours between the proverbial rock and a hard place. During that time, he slowly finished off what little food and water he had and, by the sixth day, realized that there was no chance of being found alive. So being desperate to survive, Aron took out a pocket knife and successfully cut his arm off. It was an excruciatingly painful move, but it was a necessary move. After freeing himself, he rappelled the rest of the way down to the canyon floor, and encountered a couple of hikers who helped him to get rescued by helicopter. The only way Aron Ralston was able to walk free after being stuck was by cutting off what was holding him back.

There are times in life when God wants to see if we have what it takes to cut away those things that keep us from being all that God has created us to be. There are habits, people, mindsets, world views, and past mistakes that we need to take the time to cut off. If we don't make this very painful but necessary move to cut off certain friendships, relationships and habits, we will never be able to experience the freedom that God desires for us. We have to face it. We have to cut it.

The Power of the Church

*And let us not neglect our meeting together,
as some people do but encourage one another,
especially now that the day of His return is
near. (Hebrews 10:25)*

In the movie *Fighting Temptations*, Cuba Gooding Jr. plays Darrin Hill, a big time advertising executive in New York who gets word that his Aunt Sally has passed away. Upon arriving in a small country town in Georgia, Hill discovers that his phone has no signal. He tries to use his cell phone on multiple occasions, and in multiple locations, but he is unsuccessful. On the day of the funeral, as Hill was sitting in church, his phone began to ring. Shocked that his phone finally got a signal, he came to realize that the *only* place his phone was able to get the power and connection it needed was in church.

It is said that the millennial generation is the first generation of African Americans in this country with a strong disconnect from the church. Birthed in slavery, the Black church met in secret as the people gave one another encouragement and hope during the time of dehumanization and bondage. In the midst of Jim Crow and legal segregation, the Black church took Christianity from the four walls of the church into the community and into politics in the form of the Civil Rights Movement. Today, however, times have certainly changed. No longer do the people of our community turn to the church for moral and spiritual encouragement. No longer do we rely on the church to help raise our families and build our communities. And, if we look around at our families and our community, we will see that we have lost something. The church will survive the millennial generation just as it has survived every generation before ours. But how sad it would be if history records that we were the generation willing to let it die. Our needs are so great, and the answers to our moral, spiritual, family, and community crisis can still be found in the place we think we have outgrown. If we want to be everything that God has created us to be, it is time that we get reconnected with the church, which has been the cornerstone of the Black community throughout our history.

Removing the Crookedness

Do not be misled: "Bad company corrupts good character."
(1 Corinthians 15:33)

One day I went to the dentist and was informed that I had to get a wisdom tooth removed. This was one painful experience that I didn't want to have. I tried to persuade the dentist to skip the task. However, the dentist wanted me to understand the benefit of removing my wisdom tooth. He said that I had to get my wisdom tooth removed because it was coming in crooked, causing a cavity in the straight tooth next to it. Since the crooked tooth was causing a disease on the straight tooth, the crooked tooth had to be removed.

The Bible says that bad company corrupts good character. Many of us are missing out on what God has for us, because we keep surrounding ourselves with crooked people. "Crooked" can mean dishonest or illegal, but it can also mean warped or twisted. Bad or crooked company includes people with crooked behavior and mindset; people who handle their money and raise their kids in a crooked way; and people who operate within their friendships and other relationships in a way that is crooked. However, if we allow God to operate as dentist, the God we serve has a way of removing the people, the thinking, and the behavior that is crooked in our lives in order to straighten us out so that we can grow in a healthy way. Let's remove the crookedness.

Take It Off

"Do not come any closer," God said.
"Take off your sandals, for the place
where you are standing is holy ground."
(Exodus 3:5)

My mom has the spiritual gift of interior decorating. So when it was time for me to move out on my own, I just let Mom do her thing. I was at work when the couch and chair I bought arrived at my new apartment. Once the furniture was in place, Mom called me and told that she thought the chair was too big and took too much space. I decided that once I got home, I would do a little redecorating because I really didn't want to get rid of my new chair. When I arrived home, I decided to move the chair into my bedroom to make more space in the living room. However, when I got the chair to my bedroom door, I discovered that it was too big to fit through the door! After getting in contact with my interior decorator, aka my momma, I discovered that when the movers brought the chair to my new apartment, they removed the legs from the bottom of the chair in order for it to fit through the open door.

The senior saints would say that God opens doors that no man can close. It is God who opens doors for us; it is up to us to walk through. There have been doors that God has opened up for us, but many of us can't fit through because we've got too much stuff attached to us. There was a relationship door that we missed out on because we had too much baggage attached to us. There was a career door that we didn't enter because we had too much fear attached to us. There were other doors that God wanted us to walk through but we couldn't fit because of all the sin that was attached to us. At some point, we have to allow God to be the Interior Decorator of our hearts and minds. We have to eliminate the things that need to be removed in order for us to fit through the doors that God has opened for us. Whatever it is, let's take it off.

Stay Close to the Source

If you remain in me and my words remain in you, ask whatever you wish, and it will be done for you. (John 15:7)

I think the technology of the Bluetooth is so cool. It gives one the ability to get audio from a device without any cords or wires. The only catch with any Bluetooth device is that you have to be in close proximity to the source that is feeding the sound. The closer you are to the source, the better the sound. The farther you get from the source, the more unclear the sound becomes. One afternoon as I was cleaning up my apartment, I was rockin' to some Kendrick Lamar through my new Bluetooth headphone set. I was in the zone. K. Dot was telling me everything was going to be "Alright," and I believed him. But when I began to take the trash out, I discovered the sound in my headphones was breaking up. The more I was dealing with trash, the trashier the sound became. Once I got to the dumpster, the headphones were playing no sound at all. It was then I realized that as I walked outside to take out the trash, I was getting farther and farther away from the source until I finally got disconnected. But once I put the trash away, and started walking back towards the source, I was able to hear everything with clarity.

Life makes it hard for us to hear God sometimes. We know God is communicating, but for some reason, we don't comprehend. At first, we may wonder, "What's happened to God?" But maybe it isn't God. Perhaps we have distanced ourselves from the Main Source, Christ Jesus. If we can be honest with ourselves, the distance from Christ came when we continued to move towards the trash. Making trashy choices, using trashy money management, and hanging with trashy people have caused us to miss out on what God wants to communicate through the Holy Spirit. However, despite how far we have gone, we are never so far that God's grace can't redirect us back to Him. Stay close to the Source.

Day 14

Not Always Easy With the King

"I have told you these things, so that in me you may have peace. In this world you will have trouble. But take heart! I have overcome the world."

(John 16:33)

Let's be real. When LeBron "King" James took his talents to South Beach that was probably one of the best things that could have happened in NBA history. He teamed up with Dwayne Wade and Chris Bosh, who are great athletes in their own right. They dominated the NBA for 4 years while winning two NBA championships. After doing damage in Miami, King James went back to Cleveland and won another championship in 2016. In one of his first preseason games as a Cleveland Cavalier, he played against Wade, Bosh and the Miami Heat. The game was played in Rio de Janeiro, Brazil. Before the game, reporters interviewed Chris Bosh about his time playing with LeBron James. Despite winning two championships with the king, Bosh told the reporters that at times it was difficult. He said there were many sacrifices made in order to play with the king. Not only did Bosh have to sacrifice money, he had to also sacrifice how he played the game. During his first few seasons with the Toronto Raptors, Chris Bosh scored more points and grabbed more rebounds than while he was playing with LeBron. While he fully appreciated being part of a winning team, Bosh said it was difficult making all of those sacrifices in order to play with the king.

As believers, we, too, will learn that it's not always easy playing with the King. Just because we're on the team with the King, it doesn't mean everything will be easy. Just because we're on the team with the King, it doesn't mean we won't experience valleys. Just because we're on the team with the King, it doesn't mean we won't have to make sacrifices. But Chris Bosh learned that as long as he was willing to sacrifice on behalf of the king, he could experience victory. As long as we are willing to sacrifice on behalf of King Jesus, we, too, will experience victory. In today's verse, Jesus warns us that in this life we will have tribulation, but in that same breath he encourages us and says that he has overcome the world. That's why, when things get difficult in life, we don't have to give up. We're still on the same team with the King. Regardless how bad our situation gets, the King will always come out on top, and we will be there with Him. We're on the team with the King of kings, Christ Jesus our Lord.

Time for An Audible

Seated in a window was a young man
named Eutychus, who was sinking into
a deep sleep as Paul talked on and on.
When he was sound asleep, he fell to the
ground from the third story and was
picked up dead. (Acts 20:9)

Peyton Manning is my guy! I'm a Colts fan, so I love what he did for our city both on and off the field. What I loved most about Peyton on the field was his intellect. He had a strong arm and an accurate pass, but it was his mind during the game that intrigued me the most. Peyton seemed to always know what the defense was about to do and called plays that were based off his reads. Sometimes Peyton kept the play he called in the huddle but other times he would call an audible and change the play. I loved when Peyton called an audible. An audible does not change the goal, but it changes the play the team uses to get to the goal. Peyton still wanted to score and get the victory, but based on how the defense may have been set up, Peyton would change his mind. In essence he would say that what his team had been calling had not been working, so he chose a new play that would, in fact, help them reach their goal of victory.

If truth be told, the church needs to make an audible. Based on how the opposition is after our youth, families, communities, and churches, the past plays are no longer working. It's time for the church to call an audible. We don't want to change the goal. Our mission is still to advance the kingdom of God in this world. However, we can always be innovative and creative in our approach to ministry. Let's not make the same mistake as Paul in Acts 20 and keep talking and talking until we put people to sleep. It's time to implement new ways to communicate the gospel. Whether it is through dance, visuals, rap, short films or whatever, we need to hold their attention long enough for them to hear about the love and grace of God. We've seen too many young people falling out of the church and into the streets; it's time to make a change. It's time to call an audible.

Creating in Chaos

In the beginning God created the heavens and the earth. Now the earth was formless and empty, and darkness was over the surface of the deep, and the Spirit of God was hovering over the waters. And God said, "Let there be light," and there was light. (Genesis 1:1-4)

I received my Master of Divinity degree at the Interdenominational Theological Center in Atlanta, Georgia. Atlanta is a great city; the traffic, not so much. When three inches of snow fell in the city of Atlanta in 2013, the highways were backed up for miles. The city was not used to snow at all and was not prepared for it, so even the smallest snowstorm took out the city. However, out of the chaos a story emerged about a woman who gave birth in the midst of the whole ordeal. A police officer patrolling the area came upon the pregnant woman, her husband, and their two daughters stuck in bumper-to-bumper traffic on the highway because of the storm. The father was on the phone calling 911 as the officer approached them. Soon after, the father and police officer found themselves assisting in the birth of the couple's third child. The parents named this child born in a storm "Grace."

This couple taught us a valuable life lesson. The storms of life don't give us an excuse to give up, or to become lazy, mean or evil. There are opportunities for us to birth something good even in circumstances of adversity. The history of African-Americans in this country shows us the power of creating in chaos. They were able to birth families and churches even in the midst of slavery. They were able to produce schools and communities in the face of Jim Crow and legal segregation. We come from people who built in the midst of bondage. We come from people who knew how to create in chaos. When things get tough, the grace of God is present. That grace will give us what we need to be productive and effective in the community and kingdom. God gives us the power to create in the midst of chaos.

Suffering for Glory

I consider that our present sufferings
are not worth comparing with the glory
that will be revealed in us.

(Romans 8:18)

My family and I were blessed to take a cruise around some of the islands in Hawaii. On one of the islands, we took a tour on a trail that led us to a beautiful waterfall. On our way to the waterfall, the tour guide told us about the history of Hawaii, stopping to point out some of the plants along the trail, and even handing us fruit that was safe for us to eat. She stopped at one plant, broke off a small piece, and passed it around so that we could all get a whiff of this plant's beautiful fragrance. My brothers and I were the clowns on the tour and when the tour guide handed us the plant to smell, we were tripping because we couldn't smell anything. I protested, "You told us that this plant smelled good and we can't even smell anything!" Evidently we were clowning around so much that we didn't hear the guide when she told us that before we could pick up the scent of this particular plant, we had to crush its leaves.

Our scripture today reminds us that in order for us to experience glory, there are moments of suffering that we have to endure. Just like those plants on the Hawaiian trail, God sometimes has to crush us so our special qualities can be exposed. God has instilled purpose, creativity, dreams and greatness in each one of us, and sometimes God has to send us through the crushing seasons in life so the value that He instilled in us can become apparent to others. There are times when you will feel crushed by your supervisor at work, by your professor at school, or by your family at home. It is in these moments of life that God is looking for us to endure the struggle so we can experience the glory. Let's not forget that David walked through the "valley of the shadow of death" before he was able to sit at the table in front of his enemies. Let us also not forget that Jesus was crushed by the cross before He was able to ascend to the right hand of God. Sometimes God will allow the crushing and suffering so that "the glory that will be revealed in us" will be all the more apparent. The suffering precedes the glory.

Don't Be Scared of the Dark

*As the sun was going down, Abram
fell into a deep sleep, and a terrifying
darkness came down over him. Then the
Lord said to Abram...*

(Genesis 15:12-13)

Throughout American history, as well as in other countries, people have given neutral words such as *black* or *dark* negative meanings. They are defined, for instance, in American dictionaries with such words as evil, bad, and wicked. Although some want us to attach negativity to *black* or *darkness,* in the world of photography, darkness is very useful. The darkroom in photography is a space for photographers to develop their photos. The darkroom leaves no space for light and is completely dark. That darkness is needed so that the photograph's image can develop and appear with clarity.

There will be moments in life when things get dark. The moments of darkness create a time when we might get nervous and act out in fear, but they are intended to be our opportunity to act out in faith. When things get dark in our lives, that should be a sign that God is getting ready to move. All throughout the Bible, you see God using darkness to work on behalf of His people. Genesis 1 says that it was dark before God moved, not to eliminate the darkness, but to separate the darkness from the light. Then he said that what he did was good; the darkness as well as the light was good. In Exodus 10, God used the darkness of Egypt to convince Pharaoh to let the people of God go. In Matthew 27, the Bible says that darkness covered the whole land from noon until three in afternoon as Jesus died on the cross. It was in that moment of darkness that God made possible our salvation through Christ. Regardless of how dark it may get in our lives, in our communities, or in our world, God is still moving. God will use the dark moments in our lives to speak to us, provide for us, develop us and accomplish His will for our lives. Don't be scared of the dark.

Get Ya Mind Right

Set your mind on things above.
(Colossians 3:2)

One summer, I was blessed to be a counselor at an annual camp sponsored by my home church, Eastern Star Church in Indianapolis, Indiana. Before the camp started, all of the counselors were brought in for CPR Training. The trainers brought in three different sized dummies – infant, child, and adult – to help us practice the proper way to administer CPR. They told us to remember that the most vital thing is make sure that the head is positioned right. This is true no matter the age or gender of the person who needs to receive this life-giving procedure. It doesn't matter how much air, how much breath of life, we are trying to provide to someone, that person will never be able to receive it when the head is out of position.

The reason why many of us don't receive some of the things that God is trying to give to us is because our head is out of position. God is the ultimate Giver. God gives life, love, joy and peace, but if our head is out of position we will never be able to embrace the things that God desires to give us. What's on your mind? Some of us have Jesus in our hearts but we don't have

Him in our head. We love Christ but we think like a consumer. We love the Savior, but we think like a slave. We love God but we think we don't have what it takes to succeed. However, Paul exhorts us to think of those things that are spiritual, because when our minds are positioned in Christ, we will be able to receive everything that God has for us. We each need to get our mind right.

Day 20

Stay in Bounds

*Marriage should be honored by all, and
the marriage bed kept pure, for God will
judge the adulterer and all the sexually
immoral. (Hebrews 13:4)*

I was out watching football with the homies one Sunday evening. I forget which NFL teams were playing but I will never forget this particular play. The game was close and the home team was down by four points. They were in the red zone looking to score with a few seconds left in the game. The quarterback snapped the ball and passed it to one of his best receivers. The receiver caught the ball in the end zone and the referees signaled a score. They put the points on the scoreboard. The fans went crazy. The receiver was dancing. His team was celebrating and it looked like they were going to get the victory. But because there were less than two minutes to go in the game, the officials went back to review the play. Upon further review, they discovered that before the player caught the ball for the touchdown, he stepped out of bounds. Because he crossed the boundary line, the score didn't count. The NFL has a rule, that a player who has stepped out of bounds during a play for any reason cannot come back in bounds and touch the ball. So the officials took the points off the scoreboard, the fans stop cheering, and the teammates stopped celebrating. Because the player crossed the line before scoring, the team couldn't get the full benefits of the score and missed out on victory.

The Bible says that the bed is undefiled in marriage. In other words, sexual activity is only reserved for a man and woman who are married. God created sex, and there are physical, mental, and spiritual benefits that come with sex. Some of us miss out on all the benefits that come with sex because we keep stepping out of bounds trying to score. The game is designed for us to score within the boundaries that God has set for us. Victory is won in the area of our sexuality when we play within the boundary that God has set. We must keep our activity in bounds.

Wait For the Captain

Whether the cloud stayed over the tabernacle for two days or a month or a year, the Israelites would remain in camp and not set out; but when it lifted, they would set out.

(Numbers 9:17)

I was at the Atlanta airport one day anticipating my flight back home to Indianapolis when I learned that my flight had been delayed. I looked outside and the plane was there. I looked on my phone and found that the weather seemed fair from Atlanta to Indianapolis. I decided to talk to the airline representative at the counter to investigate why my trip was being delayed. When I asked her, she told me that the delay had nothing to do with the plane; the plane was at the gate and ready to fly. She even assured me that the weather was perfect for flying. The reason for the delay was that the captain had not yet arrived. Moments after speaking to the airline representative, I saw the captain coming around the corner with his crew. Once the captain and his crew got settled on board the plane, we were all able to board the plane and get to our final destination.

To pursue purpose without Christ is like a passenger trying to get to a destination without the captain. I admit that in my eagerness to reach certain goals, there have been times that I have taken off without the Captain—and have ended up going nowhere. Pursuing purpose without the Captain only increases the chance of crashing and burning before reaching our destiny. It is the Captain who is trained and skilled in getting the passengers to their destination safely. Yet, even though we know that Christ is our Captain, we may still sometimes feel that we are being delayed in getting to what God has for us. It may appear as if other people are taking off before us. Our friends are getting married and our colleagues are advancing in their careers, and we feel that we are still waiting to take off. During our delay, we may *feel* that God is denying us our destiny; but God's delay is not a denial. He knows the best time for us to take off; He knows how to avoid turbulence; and He knows the exact time that we need to arrive. It's better to be patient and wait for the power of Christ to guide us than to take off by ourselves and fall short of what God has for us. Let us wait for the Captain.

Praise Him in Chains

But about midnight Paul and Silas were
praying and singing hymns of praise to God,
and the prisoners were listening to them; and
suddenly there came a great earthquake, so
that the foundations of the prison house were
shaken; and immediately all the doors were
opened and everyone's chains were unfastened.
(Acts 16:22-26)

In 2000, the musical duo *Mary Mary* stormed on the scene with the song "Shackles." This song had a major influence in the progression of gospel music. I remember growing up in church hearing this song everywhere—from the gospel night at the skating rink to all the youth conferences! It seemed that every dance team had a routine to this song. It was a big hit among church folk. But as I read this story about Paul and Silas I realized that I have theological issues with some of the lyrics. The lyrics read:

Take the shackles off my feet so I can dance
I just wanna praise you
I just wanna praise you
You broke the chains now I can lift my hands

And I'm gonna praise you
I'm gonna praise you

Modern day Christianity has sometimes been guilty of putting conditions on our relationship with God. I know I have personally been guilty of thinking things such as, "If God doesn't do this, I won't do that," or "If God won't show up when I need Him, then I'm taking matters into my own hands." In a similar spirit, this song suggests that we wait for our shackles to come off and chains to be broken before we give praise to God. However, Paul and Silas encourage us not to wait until our situation improves before we give God praise. In fact, the only reason why the Black church exists today is because its founding mothers and fathers didn't wait until their chains were broken before they praised God. Even though it was forbidden for most of those in slavery to attend church, my ancestors got together in secret and they prayed, praised, and worshiped God. They didn't wait until their situation got better. They let God know that they loved Him, trusted Him, and counted Him worthy of praise even when they were still in the midst of their suffering. We can learn from their example, and from the example of Paul and Silas. We don't have to wait to be free before we give God praise. The character of God remains good, even when our circumstances are bad. So despite our mental, emotional, physical, and spiritual shackles, God still deserves all praise. And God is moved by our praise. Praising God in bondage ignites the Spirit of God to move on our behalf. We must praise God despite the chains.

Get the Update

And we all, who with unveiled faces contemplate the Lord's glory, are being transformed into His image with ever-increasing glory, which comes from the Lord, who is the Spirit.

(2 Corinthians 3:18)

Apple technology has taken over the world since its release of the Apple iPhone. Not only have their designs evolved over the years, but the programming within the devices has evolved. To keep the phones they sold in synch with their continually changing programming, periodically Apple sends its users a software update. The software update is designed to enhance the technology that allows the iPhone to be the iPhone. The software update that Apple provides fixes problems and enhances the device from the inside. One day as I was trying to upload the new software update to my iPhone 6, a notification popped up on my screen that informed me that my battery was too low to get the update. The notification also came with a suggestion. It said that if I wanted to successfully upload the new software update, I needed to get connected to a power source.

God's power, through the Holy Spirit, has updates available for our marriages, relationships, friendships, finances, and careers. The problem is we keep missing out because we are trying to obtain the power, but we are disconnected from Christ. Whenever we try to operate in life while disconnected from our source of power in Christ Jesus, we will never have what it takes to experience the spiritual updates that God has available for us. If truth be told, our communities, families, churches, schools, and political systems also need updates. The only way we can make that happen is if we get connected to our source of power in Christ Jesus, and let Him work through us to help reconnect our systems. Thank God that He has updates available for us. It's time to get the update.

From Brokenness to Blessings

Then Jacob was left alone, and a man wrestled with him until daybreak. When he saw that he had not prevailed against him, he touched the socket of his thigh; so the socket of Jacob's thigh was dislocated while he wrestled with him. Then he said, "Let me go, for the dawn is breaking." But he said, "I will not let you go unless you bless me." So he said to him, "What is your name?" And he said, "Jacob." He said, "Your name shall no longer be Jacob, but Israel; for you have striven with God and with men and have prevailed." Then Jacob asked him and said, "Please tell me your name." But he said, "Why is it that you ask my name?" And he blessed him there. (Genesis 32:22-32)

In 1993, the movie *Rookie of the Year* took over the Johnson household. My brothers and I had that movie on repeat for hours. We watched it—no, studied it—until we learned each line word for word. Still to this day, you can catch us tuned in to *Rookie of the Year*. The movie is about a 12-year-old boy named Henry, who had dreams of playing Major League Baseball. Despite how big his dreams were, Henry wasn't very skilled in the game. He barely made his peewee baseball team.

But one day when trying to impress a girl at his school during recess, Henry tripped over a baseball, landed in a peculiar position, and broke his arm. After being in a cast for six weeks, the doctor informed Henry and his mother that the arm healed in a very interesting way. The way his arm healed enabled Henry to have extreme power in his arm. He could now throw a baseball faster than most professional MLB pitchers. The Chicago Cubs ended up signing this 12-year-old phenomenon and Henry was able to lead his team to the World Series. But the only reason he was able to enjoy one victory after another was because Henry endured some brokenness. Had it not been for the brokenness, he never would have been able to live out his dream.

God has great things in store for us but sometimes He has to take us through a season of brokenness. There are some things that God has waiting for us, but He first wants to see how we handle the broken moments in life. In fact, it is the moments of brokenness that will help us better appreciate the blessing when it comes. The broken relationships help us appreciate the healthy ones. The broken friendships help us appreciate the loyal ones. Our broken way of life, enables us to be open for something new. Sometimes God will break us before God can bless us. We can then use our brokenness as a testimony to bless someone else in a season of brokenness. We are not blessed in spite of our brokenness; we are blessed *because* we have been broken.

Bad Hand, Good Partner

Then he said to the man, "Stretch out your hand." So he stretched it out and it was completely restored, just as the other one. (Matt 12:10, 13)

A family get-together is not really official until the card game Spades is played. Spades is something serious. If you don't play, don't sit at the table. I remember when I was playing Spades with my brother Jordan, my cousin Daniel, and our homie Tre. Tre and Daniel were partners while I partnered with Jordan. In Spades, the number one rule is that you can't talk across the table. However, my brother and I had code words we liked to use in an attempt to let each other know what type of hand we were working with. Throughout the entire game my brother Jordan complained about how bad his hand was. He would tell me that he had a *bloody* hand, which means that he got a hand full of diamonds and hearts. Or he would tell me that he was "headed to the club later that night," which means he got a hand full of clubs. Despite how bad his hand was, we won one round after another. At the end of the game, Jordan and I came out with the ultimate victory. My auntie, who was in the kitchen overhearing the competitiveness of the game, asked Jordan, "How did you win if your hand was so bad?" Jordan responded by saying, "Easy, I had a good partner."

Life at times has a way of dealing out bad hands. You were a product of a single parent household; that's a bad hand. You experienced a divorce; that's a bad hand. You got laid off from your job; that's a bad hand. The African-American community has been the victim of an evil social system; we've been dealt a bad hand. If we are not careful, we will internalize the words of society or of Pharisaic church folk. They often tell us that we will not be able to reach what God has for us because of our bad hand. But even though we may have been dealt a bad hand, as long as we can partner up with our Big Brother Jesus, we will be able to get the victory despite how bad the hand we were dealt. A bad hand means nothing with a Good Partner.

Let the Son Return

Here I am! I stand at the door and knock. If anyone hears my voice and opens the door, I will come in and eat with that person and they with me. (Rev. 3:20)

I am a product of Disney movies. My brothers and I had a heavy dose of Disney growing up in the Johnson household. We had all the classics: *Aladdin, Beauty and the Beast*, and, of course, my favorite, *The Lion King. The Lion King* is great! All the characters added something special to the story but Simba had such a strong influence on me. Simba and I have similar stories. We are both first-born sons of our fathers who are influential leaders in their communities. I can totally feel where Simba was coming from in that regard. But Simba has so much dysfunction in his family that he decides to run away from home after his Uncle Scar convinces him that he killed his own father. When Simba runs off, Scar becomes king of Pride Rock and the whole community suffers. The community begins to experience what happens when the son is absent. Animals were getting sick, there was no growth in the land, and not enough food for the tribes—all because the son was absent. After a certain turn of events, Simba returns home and becomes king of Pride Rock. When the son returned, peace and order were brought back to the community.

It is time for the Black community to allow the Son of God to return back into our homes and families. Narcissism, self-hatred, and the destruction of the Black family are just a few of the symptoms that express themselves when the community gets away from the Son. When the Black community was centered on Christ, there was nothing that we couldn't endure and overcome. During the times of slavery, it was illegal for Black people to have church. However, the Black church emerged out of a context of oppression and it was the Black preachers like Nat Turner and Harriet Tubman who centered what they did on Christ. They not only preached freedom and equality to the people of God but they were willing to give their lives for the people they served. It was the Black church centered on the Son that ignited the Civil Rights Movement and enabled the rights that many people experience today. Sadly, our children today want to be more like celebrities than like God. Our preachers have become more Hollywood minded than Kingdom minded. Our families are no longer stable. We are experiencing the negative effects of a community where the Son of God is absent. The Bible says that Christ is knocking, and it is time that we, individually and communally, let Him in. We need to let the Son return.

Connected at the Top

Remain in me as I remain in you.
(John 15:4)

Before the start of my last year of seminary in Atlanta, I moved in with my friend Tim. Tim is the only person I have known who was so adamant about cutting back on his electricity bill that he unplugged every electric device in the apartment, even when it was turned off. Whenever Tim was done watching TV, using the printer, or using the light of a lamp, he would unplug it. The first month or so after moving in, I was still getting use to the *unplug rule*. One day I was trying to get connected to the Wi-Fi Internet, but for some reason it wasn't working for me. Frustrated, I called Tim to let him know that his Internet wasn't working. He assured me that nothing was wrong. He told me that before he left, he unplugged the wireless router. My room was in the basement. Tim informed me that in order for me to connect with the Wi-Fi, I had to go upstairs to his office and plug in what had been disconnected. So I did just that. I got out of the basement, went to the top floor, and reconnected what had been disconnected. I was able then to access what I needed after getting plugged in at the top.

I remember the days when I tried to access certain things in life but I couldn't get them. I tried to access wholeness, purpose, and fulfillment, but kept coming up short. This continued until, finally, I realized that I couldn't access peace of mind or any of these things I desired because I was disconnected from the Source of all these things. Somehow, I had allowed the circumstances of life to disconnect me from God. Today, let us commit to taking our life to the next level and get reconnected with God. Once we get connected to God, we will again have the power to access the love, joy, peace and spirit we need in our lives. It's time for us to get out of our comfort zone, take our relationship with God to the next level, and experience a life that's connected at the top.

Never Too Low

For you know the grace of our Lord Jesus Christ, that though He was rich, yet for your sake He became poor, so that you through His poverty might become rich. (2 Corinthians 8:9)

Not long ago, I came across a news story that took place in December 2013. A tugboat traveling off the coast of Nigeria had sunk 100 feet below sea level, along with the entire 12-man crew. Three days passed before the investigative divers went down to collect the bodies. As they arrived at the sunken ship, they discovered that not everyone died. There was a cook on board the ship named Harrison Okene who had survived the terrible accident. After the ship sank, Harrison somehow landed in an air pocket inside one of the cabins. Harrison said he was able to survive three days in that air pocket because of Coca-Cola and prayer. Harrison testifies that he knew the situation was virtually hopeless. It was totally dark; the water was cold; the oxygen in the air pocket was dwindling; the salt water began to tear at his flesh; and he was all alone. He said, "I was on the edge of life and death, and I knew the only thing that could save me is the grace of God." Harrison was right. The grace of God came to the rescue when one of the divers went down 100 feet into the murky water and got Harrison out of something that he couldn't get out of by himself.

There are times when we can find ourselves low down. Low down in depression, in our finances, or even in sin. In these times, we are in such low-down predicaments that we can't save ourselves. But God isn't a god who sits idly by and doesn't get involved in human affairs. In fact, God in Jesus Christ came all the way down from heaven to earth to get us out of sin, something we couldn't overcome ourselves. We now have the power to live a life that is pleasing to God, because Jesus took on the low-down disposition of flesh in order for us to experience the life and nature of Christ. So no matter how low down we have gone, we can never be too low down that Christ can't raise us up.

Ant Sense

Go to the ant, you sluggard; consider its ways and be wise. (Proverbs 6:6)

In 2015, a terrible storm took place near South Carolina which led to days of flooding. Many people died and others were injured, while thousands had to deal with power outages all throughout the state. In the midst of the flood, there was a picture and video that went viral. It showed thousands of fire ants coming together and creating what looked like a floating raft. Fire ants have shells that are resistant to water, and when they come across floods, or any horrible situation that might take them out, they come together and float for long distances in order to survive. While people were dying because of the flood, these fire ants understood that the only way they could survive was by coming together.

"Ubuntu" is a Southern African term upon which a philosophy has been built that recognizes, "I am because we are." Our survival as humanity is not based on how well we do individually or the things we attain for ourselves. Our survival is determined by how effectively we can come together. Our family, communities, and churches are under attack by narcissistic values and ideas that are saturating our society. Leviticus 26:8 says, "And five of you shall chase an hundred, and an hundred of you shall put ten thousand to flight." Alone, we can do little. But if we learn from the ant, we will see that the only way for us to overcome the things that are trying to take us out is by coming together to fight side by side for the destiny of our families and communities. Let us get some ant sense.

The Testimony of a Chipotle Napkin

Therefore, if anyone be in Christ, he is a new creation. (2 Corinthians 5:17)

My youngest brother KJ used to love going to Chipotle. I was never in love with Chipotle like KJ, but the summer before his freshman year at Howard University, I made it a priority to spend more time with him. So if KJ wanted Chipotle, then we were going to Chipotle. One particular time we were there, I just happened to read the back of the napkin and, to my surprise, the napkin spoke to me. It was like a testimony. On the back of the napkin was an explanation about where the napkin came from. Evidently Chipotle uses recycled paper to make their napkins. Their napkins are 90% recycled paper, and the back of the napkin *testified* that it used to be a parking ticket or an electric bill until it was used and thrown away. But I was able to read the testimony of the napkin that day because somebody took what was thrown away, recycled it, and created something else useful out of it.

The church ought to be a recycling bin for human beings. The church ought to be a place for people who have been thrown away, tossed aside, rejected, or abused, because God is the ultimate Recycler. God has a way of taking us as we are and making us into what God wants us to be. I know many people in church like to play 'super holy' and act like they always have been connected with God. But in all honesty, the church is intended to be a recycling bin for people who are tired of being in trouble, who are done with unhealthy relationships, or who are frustrated with being empty inside. We all have a Chipotle napkin testimony. We used to be something that was thrown away, but God came along and made us into something that can bring God glory.

A Killer Past

But Lot's wife looked back, and she became a pillar of salt. (Genesis 19:26)

In 2015, the *Chicago Tribune* reported about an 87-year-old man from Chicago who died from a gunshot wound he got in the 1940s as a teenager. The medical examiner said that Tom Buchanan died from complications in the abdomen, caused by this 70-year-old bullet wound. According to his doctors, a bullet left inside a body has a way of breaking down over time. The body then absorbs the fragments of the bullet causing problems even years after the incident occurred. The medical examiner said that Mr. Buchanan died as an adult from something he didn't address as a teenager.

Psychologists suggest that many of the mental and emotional problems we face as adults stem from what happened to us in our childhood. There are many cases where people fail to address the abuse, neglect, and rejection they received as children. Failure to address the issues and baggage of the past has a way of causing deadly problems in the present. Many of our relationships, friendships, and dreams die because of issues we failed to address when we first encountered them. However, the God we serve is the same today, yesterday and forevermore. God has enough power and grace to help us deal with our past issues in a healthy way. That may include prayer, fasting, talking with a pastor, and seeking the assistance of a counselor or therapist. Some people are too proud to admit that they need help, so they eventually die—emotionally, mentally, spiritually, and sometimes even physically—because of their untreated wounds. We must be open to the mental, emotional and spiritual help that God has available for us, so that our past won't cause us to miss out on the future that God has planned. Beware of the killer past.

Superman Faith

*I can do all things through Christ.
(Philippians 4:13)*

Superheroes had a major role in raising the Johnson Boys. My father still has an insatiable love of superhero movies and comic books. The love for the art of superhero storytelling was then passed on to his four sons. One of my favorite superheroes of all time is the great Superman. Superman is super cool. If you haven't heard, Superman is "faster than a speeding bullet," and his strength, makes him "more powerful than a locomotive." Superman was unstoppable—until he ran across kryptonite. Kryptonite was Superman's only weakness. There would be times when Superman's enemies would get the best of him with their use of kryptonite. There would be moments when I thought it would be over for Superman after his weakness has been exposed. However, even though his weakness was in kryptonite, his strength was found in the sun and all Superman needed was exposure to the sun to get his energy restored. It was the sun that strengthened him to get the victory over his enemies.

Life has a way of making us feel weak. Friends disappoint, finances disappear, and families become dysfunctional. Life has a way of getting the best of us. We can't give up in those moments of despair and defeat. We must have Superman faith. In the times that we are weak, we must expose our lives to the Son of God. The Son has the power that we need to deal with our enemies. The Son has the energy we need to overcome our obstacles. The Son has the Spirit we need for strength, as we walk into the greatness that has been destined for us. We must have a little Superman faith, and get in the Son.

Daddy Knows Best

*But Jonah ran away from the Lord and
headed for Tarshish...Now the Lord
provided a huge fish to swallow Jonah,
and Jonah was in the belly of the fish
three days and three nights.*

(Jonah 1:3, 17)

Our Young Adult Ministry at Eastern Star Church had a
cookout at a local park. As we were setting up, there was a
family reunion taking place in the same area. I was walking
to my car to collect a few things, and saw a father and his
toddler daughter walking in front of me. They were coming
from the playground and the daughter was full of energy and
enthusiasm. The grass was still muddy from the storm the day
before and the father warned his daughter to stay close to him
on the sidewalk. However, the daughter, full of excitement,
paid no mind to her father and continued to run along in the
grass. The father again told the child to come walk with him
because he didn't want her to get dirty. Again, the daughter
paid no attention to the father and continued to run in the grass
until she tripped and fell in one of the muddiest spots in the

area. The father was frustrated. In tears, his young daughter learned a lesson that day: the farther she gets away from her father, the dirtier life becomes.

I can admit that there are times when *my* Father wanted me to talk and walk with Him, and I ignored him. I ignored His signs, His people, and His Word. As a result of rejecting the command of my Father, my life got a little dirty. I made dirty decisions, spent my money in dirty ways, and did dirty things to people I cared about. But despite how dirty life gets, the Father never gives up on His children. Just like the frustrated father at the park, God has a way of going into the mud and dirt with us to bring us out. Walking with the Father is not always easy, but His grace has a way of making us clean. Daddy knows best.

From Barren to Productive

A certain man of Zorah, named Manoah, from the clan of the Danites, had a wife who was childless, unable to give birth. The angel of the Lord appeared to her and said, "You are barren and childless, but you are going to become pregnant and give birth to a son." (Judges 13:2-3)

While it has not yet happened successfully in the United States, five babies in Sweden have been born to women who were themselves born without a uterus. These miracles happened because a team of doctors there discovered how to transplant a uterus from a deceased donor into the body of a healthy woman. These women did not have the opportunity to produce before, but they were given the ability to procreate after making a necessary change on the inside.

In the spiritual realm, we tend to look for external reasons to determine why we aren't producing at the level we need to. We need to express more love, kindness, grace, and forgiveness to others. We need to win more people to Christ. We need to have happier families, more fulfilling marriages, more evangelical churches, and more unified communities. We try desperately to identify what it is that might account for our inability to produce, but still we remain barren. But when we let the Great Physician look inside of us, He can not only pinpoint the very cause of our problem, but He can also operate within us to make whatever changes are necessary. God is in the business of performing spiritual transplants. He can take us from barren to productive.

The Power is in the SON

You, God, are awesome in your sanctuary;
the God of Israel gives power and strength
to His people. (Psalm 68:35)

Pixar changed the animation industry with the 1995 classic film, *Toy Story*. By now, there are three films in the series with word that a fourth one is on the way. But regardless of how many Toy Story movies Pixar produces, the first one will always be my favorite. *Toy Story* is centered on the toys of a boy name Andy. Andy's toys have the ability to come to life. Out of all the toys that Andy possessed, Woody and Buzz Lightyear were his favorites, but they were also enemies of each other. Woody was so jealous of Buzz that he created an incident that kicked Buzz out of Andy's bedroom window. Now Woody is on a mission to go find Buzz and bring him back home before Andy and his family pack everything into the moving van and head to a new house. Woody's mission was successful and by the end of the movie, Woody and Buzz have not only reconnected, but they are now best friends. But now, all the other toys are on the moving van headed in the direction of Andy's new house, and Woody and Buzz are on a remote-controlled car in pursuit of the moving van. Then, all of a sudden, the remote- controlled car's batteries die. They are both distraught. But then they remembered that Buzz had a rocket strapped on him from earlier in the movie. In fact, it was Sid, the enemy, who gave them the tools they were going to use to reconnect with their family. Woody takes his only match and lights it to ignite the rocket. But a car goes by and the fire goes out. So now Woody and Buzz are disconnected from their love ones, with no power, and no fire. However, as Woody is crying he notices that the sun is reflecting through the glass of Buzz's helmet. So he takes the end of the rocket and aligns it with the sun, and the sun gives them everything they need to get to where they are going.

There are times in our lives when we, too, seem to be disconnected from what God wants us to do and even where He wants us to be. There are times where we may seem powerless, lose our fire, and lose our energy. In those moments of frustration, it's easy to give up and throw in the towel on our relationships, friendships, families, and dreams. But at some point, we need to make a Woody and Buzz move. No matter how drastic things are, we can always align ourselves with the Son. Let's choose this day to line up our family, relationships, money, dreams, career, and every other area of our lives with the Son of God. Then let's watch the Son give us the power and energy we need to get to the destiny God has in store for us. The power is in the Son.

"All I Need is Jesus to Win"

But thanks be to God! He has given us victory through our Lord Jesus Christ.

(1 Corinthians 15:57)

One year, as a summer camp counselor for Eastern Star Church, a few other counselors and I came up with the idea of having the children create their own bingo cards. I had the privilege of overseeing the 5-7 year olds, and these children had tons of energy that couldn't be harnessed in a classic bingo game. Instead, we had a list of terms from 5 different categories that included super heroes, colors, food, numbers and Bible characters that the children could choose from to create their bingo cards. Once the cards were created, it was my job to call out the terms from the 5 categories. So I would call out things like "red," "pizza," and "Moses." After a while, the children felt that they needed to give me their suggestions on what I should call. They would say, "Call out yellow," or "Call out Spider Man," or "Call out 3!" As their boards begin to fill up, they continued to tell me what they needed to win the game. They would say things like, "Mr. Johnson, all I need is blue to win," or, "All I need is cheeseburger to win." Then I heard one of the campers say, "All I need is Jesus to win!"

Society will have us think that everything but Jesus will put us in position to be satisfied. Sex, money, drugs, and material possessions are all put in front of Jesus as suggested vehicles to reach the destination of happiness and satisfaction. However, we all know celebrities and others who had a plethora of money, drugs, and material possessions but still felt miserable—at times, even to the point of suicide. Earthly possessions are nice but they can't satisfy the spirit. Spiritual satisfaction can only happen with Jesus. All we need is Jesus to win.

Temporary Shutdown

He says, "Be still and know that I am
God." (Psalm 46:10)

While living in Atlanta, the complex that I moved into with my friend Tim sent us an email saying that they were shutting down the water supply for a temporary period of time. They explained that throughout the week different units were having trouble with the flow of the water. The water pressure was very low, causing the flow of the water to not work effectively. So the complex thought it would be good idea to have a temporary shutdown in order to fix the flow of the water. During this time, even though we needed to take showers and wash clothes, we couldn't because the water flow wasn't right. But during the temporary shutdown, the complex was able to determine the cause of the problem and fix the issue.

We live in a society where we are constantly plugged in. We stay plugged into the latest hashtag, trending topic, TV episode, movie, and celebrity gossip. With the variety of outlets that we are plugged into, it makes it hard to hear God and follow the flow of the Spirit. It's not the fact that God isn't moving, but maybe we can't experience God because we are constantly plugged into the things of the world. We are missing out on of the flow of the Spirit. At some point, we need to have a temporary shutdown. A temporary shutdown gives us an opportunity to get in tune with God and get in touch with the flow of the Spirit. A temporary shutdown of the phone, TV, Netflix, and social media gives our hearts, minds and souls an opportunity to hear from God and walk into the place that the Spirit has for us. I heard someone say that "silence is the incubator for the soul." Silence allows us to hear the voice of God. For His sake, and for our own, let's have a temporary shutdown.

Divine Identity

*Know that the Lord is God. It is He who
made us, and we are His; we are His
people, the sheep of His pasture.*

(Psalm 100:3)

My brother Jalon and I are roommates now. One day I walked into our apartment while talking to our father on the phone, and found Jalon in search of his passport. We were leaving the country soon for our family vacation and Jalon was searching through everything trying to find his passport. As I walked in, I could tell that he had been looking for a while, but to no avail. After Jalon discovered that I was on the phone with our father, he asked me if I could ask our dad if he had seen his passport. My father assured Jalon that he had his passport. Jalon had been searching for his authorized identification in order to get to a predetermined destination. The problem was he was searching in all the wrong places. It wasn't until he connected to our father through his big brother that he was able to obtain his identity.

Many people in our churches and communities deal with an identity crisis. They have lost their sense of self and have looked for themselves in all the wrong places. They have tried to find a sense of identity in social media, drugs, alcohol, sexual relationships, and material possessions only to come out empty-handed. However, it is God who has made us and not we ourselves. Our identity is found in the Divinity. Once we connect to the Father through our Big Brother Jesus, we will be able to tap into our divine identity—who we are *in Christ*, not apart from Him.

We Fall Down, But We Get Up

For everyone has sinned; we all fall short of God's glorious standard. Yet God, with undeserved kindness, declares that we are righteous. He did this through Christ Jesus when He freed us from the penalty for our sins. (Romans 3:23-24)

My dad came across a story once about a student who fell out of bed at Iowa State. We've probably all fallen out of bed at least once; well, I certainly have. But the reason that the story of a woman falling out of bed made national news is because when she fell out of her bed, she landed outside, three stories down, on the ground in front of her dorm. One of her fellow students in the dorm overheard her calling for help, found her, called 911, and the fallen student was rushed to the hospital. Since most of us have fallen out of bed without sustaining any injuries, we can conclude that the woman wasn't injured simply because she fell out of bed. She was injured because of where she was positioned when the fall occurred—next to a screened-in window in a third-floor dorm room.

Paul reminds us in Romans that we all fall short. All of us have fallen short of God's standards. Humanity is a fallen people. The fact that we have fallen isn't the issue. The question is: where are we positioned when the fall takes place? Jesus Christ has paid the penalty for our sin so, if we are in Him when we fall, we don't fall out of God. The grace of God allows us to land in His divine forgiveness, love, and salvation. We need to get in the habit of recognizing our position in Christ by reading the right books, listening to the right people, and hearing the right music. When we know deep in our spirits that we belong to God and our hearts are turned towards Him, when a fall takes place, we know that we have not fallen out of God's loving hand, and that we still belong to Him. The important thing then is not to wallow in our own sense of guilt and self-condemnation, but to ask for God's forgiveness and then get back up. It isn't time to sit on the sidelines feeling that we aren't worthy to serve God. We thank God for His grace and faithfulness, and we continue being about our Father's business. We fall down, but we get up.

Delete the Old to Receive the New

See, I am doing a new thing! Now it springs up; do you not perceive it? I am making a way in the wilderness and streams in the wasteland. (Isaiah 43:9)

I got my undergrad degree in mass communications from Paine College, an Historically Black College and University (HBCU) in Augusta, Georgia. One of the things I hated when it came to pursuing my educational goals was working with groups. Whenever the professor put us in groups for a project, there would always be one person who planned on getting a good grade without doing any work. I remember in one particular group, I was given the responsibility of doing research online. My job was to retrieve the information, put it in an outline, and send it to the next person who was to turn it into a PowerPoint. The only problem was that when I sent the outline to that partner, he claimed that he didn't get it! Graduation was on the line and I wasn't going to fail because of the irresponsible actions of someone else. So the next day, I saw my fellow group member on campus from a distance and ran up to him to *make sure* that he received my email. I pulled out my phone and resent it to him right there on the spot. He pulled out his phone and waited for the email to arrive, but to our surprise and dismay, his phone received nothing. Then he remembered that this situation happened to him once before. He said, "I bet the reason I can't get your email is because I have too many old emails taking up space." And the moment he began to delete old messages, he started to receive the current messages that he needed in order to succeed.

God is a God of freshness and newness. There are many times when God wants to give us new relationships, new friendships, and new opportunities. But we miss out on them because we are holding onto the old. We can't expect for God to walk us into the newness of tomorrow if we continue to hold on to the dullness of yesterday. At some point, we must delete old friendships, relationships, and mindsets in order to receive the newness that God wants for our lives. It's time for us to delete the old and receive the new.

NOTES

NOTES

NOTES

NOTES

CPSIA information can be obtained
at www.ICGtesting.com
Printed in the USA
FFOW05n2301010817

9 780998 669618